D1431903

Published by: **ADLER SCHOOL OF PROFESSIONAL PSYCHOLOGY** 65 East
Wacker Placc, Suite 2100
Chicago, Il 60601 - 7298
(312) 201-5900 • fax (312) 201-5917
1st Printing 1995
2nd Printing 1999

ADLERIAN THEORY

AN INTRODUCTION

By Eva Dreikurs Ferguson, Ph.D.

To Rudolf Dreikurs

TABLE OF CONTENTS

FOREWORD

This little book is written to introduce the reader to the basic principles of Adlerian psychology in a simplified and condensed form. Many persons have expressed a need for such a book. Although at first glance Adlerian theory appears simple, on closer inspection it is evident that the theory has great depth. Courses in Adlerian theory have been found to be very helpful for practitioners in many fields, and students have expressed a need for a condensed and simplified introduction.

The present book is based largely on material given in a series of lectures on Adlerian theory at the Rudolf Dreikurs Summer School, sponsored by the International Committee of Adlerian Summer Schools and Institutes (ICASSI), in Bad Gastein, Austria, in the summer of 1982.

This book is intended to supplement the two books on Adlerian theory written by Dreikurs: *Fundamentals of Adlerian Psychology,* first printed in German in the 1930s and later in English in an American edition in 1950; and *Grundbegriffe der Individualpsychologie,* which was a revision of the earlier book and published by Klett Verlag in German in 1969.

Special acknowledgement and a sense of gratitude go to a number of persons: First, to my father, Rudolf Dreikurs, from whom I learned Adlerian psychology before I could even talk. Second, to the many ICASSI students, faculty, and Board members, who stimulated my thinking and supported my teaching of Adlerian theory, and a very special thanks goes to "Tee" Dreikurs for her loving encouragement and support. Third, to my husband, G.W. (Bill) Linden, who taped and transcribed my 1982 lectures and whose continued encouragement, support, and editorial suggestions helped to make this book a reality. Finally, thanks for their valuable comments go to my official board of editors, Bronia Grunwald, Mim Pew, Albrecht Schottky, and Achi Yotam, and a special note of appreciation is expressed to Theo Schoenaker, who printed the first edition of this book and who arranged to have it translated from English to German.

CHAPTER I

INTRODUCTION

This book presents the basic theory of Alfred Adler's Individual Psychology. A historical perspective will help clarify the unique ideas Adler presented.

At the turn of the century Adler was a physician with a general practice. During this time many physicians as well as the public at large still held dualistic beliefs regarding body versus mind and reason versus emotion. However, Adler in the early 1900s recognized that weakness in organs of the body (which he called "organ inferiority") had psychological significance in many cases. In 1902 he joined the psycho-analytic group that met with Freud, and in the ensuing years he became increasingly concerned with psychological processes. Adler was an active member of Freud's group for several years. However, before long he came to have fundamentally different views from Freud, regarding the nature of human motivation and behavior. In 1911 he left Freud's circle, and between 1911 and 1914 he strengthened his own school of thought which he called Individual Psychology. More information about this early period of Adler's work can be found in books by Bottome (1957), Orgler (1973), and Way (1962).

By the 1920s Adler had formulated a systematic body of ideas and practical applications that helped persons in all walks of life. He became highly regarded as a psychiatrist and as a specialist working with children. Until his death in 1937, he continued to develop his theory and to expand his professional influence.

Adler's Individual Psychology is a personality theory that is social-psychological, developmental, and cognitive. From the outset the theory had unique and basic concepts, but although some concepts remained unchanged between 1912 and 1937, the theory nevertheless evolved in three identifiable stages.

During the first period Adler related organ inferiority to psychological processes. He saw that organ deficiencies in themselves do not determine behavior, but that some persons can turn the deficiency into compensatory achievements while other persons become functionally weak and debilitated. He considered these individual differences as reflecting a creative process and freedom of choice. Later, in the second period of his theoretical formulations, he focused less on organ inferiorities and more on feeling of inferiority. This feeling was a subjective process and not dependent on organic events. By referring to feeling, Adler meant an outlook and an attitude and not merely emotion or sensation. During these two periods in developing his theory Adler emphasized striving to overcome: first, to overcome organ inferiority, and later, to overcome feelings of inferiority.

For some of the time in the second period he considered that a fundamental and universal human motivation was "the will to power" and that this was a primary means of overcoming feelings of inferiority. However, for the most part he focused on a more general striving for superiority than merely the striving for power. At this time he emphasized personal "minus" feelings that were overcome by striving for personal "plus" attainments. This was changed in the third period, in the late 1920s to the time of his death in 1937. In the third period Adler minimized the importance of personal striving for superiority, which is a vertical social process. Instead, as Lydia Sicher (1955) pointed out, he emphasized a horizontal social striving for equality and cooperation. He focused on a sense of identity with human society, and went beyond a concern with personal "minus" and personal "plus." In the third period Adler said the fundamental motivation of all individuals is "to belong" to the human community: to have a place, and to contribute to the welfare of human society. A more full description of this development in Adler's thinking can be found in books by Dreikurs on Adlerian theory (1950/1953, 1969) and on *Social Equality* (1971/1983), as well as in a paper by Ferguson (1984).

To summarize: In the early nineteen hundreds, when he was a physician helping patients with sick bodies, Adler developed a psychological theory that was based on organ inferiority. A broader theory, developed between approximately 1910 and 1920, focused on personality and child development and on ways the individual can strive to overcome feelings of inferiority. In the late 1920s and until 1937 he focused on the fundamental need of every person to belong to the human community and to feel he or she has a place. He postulated that *individual* striving was to contribute, whereas *society* strives from a minus to a plus and towards an ideal of perfection. Upward striving thus characterizes the group, while horizontal striving based on equality and cooperation is the potential inherent within all individuals. Only when the individual does not feel he has a place and can contribute will the individual, based on mistaken beliefs, strive to overcome feelings of inferiority by striving for superiority.

The name Individual Psychology refers to the indivisible whole of each person. Every person is an "individuum" who functions as a whole being. The name of Adler's psychology was not intended to imply an antagonism to social processes and social psychology, nor to pit the individual against society. Quite the contrary, Adler embraced the interdependence between the individual and society. The name was intended to focus on the wholeness of the individual at a time when others, especially Freud, emphasized a divided personality, with parts of the person presumed to be in internal struggle within the individual. For Adler the personality was not made up of separate parts, but rather, the person as a whole orients himself to an outer world. This emphasis on *holism* in Individual Psychology reflects a fundamental aspect of the theory.

The unity of personality that provides the wholeness was called *Life Style*. This is a technical term to describe the basic unitary and unique direction which the individual seeks in life, and thus Life Style in Adler's meaning is not to be confused with the contemporary use of that term. The latter suggests a mode of living (life style) that is changeable with time and circumstances. The contemporary term represents a fairly superficial and behavioral mode of relating to the environment, which is the opposite of what Adler meant by Life Style. Adler's meaning did not refer to a temporary or superficial mode of living but to a person's long-term orientation over his or her life span. Additionally, Life Style refers to a person's basic concepts of self and others and to the person's basic life goal.

The concept of holism and unity of personality reflects a fundamental principle of Individual

Psychology. A second basic principle is Adler's formulation that all *human behavior is purposive* and that one can understand the meaning of behavior only by understanding the individual's goals. Adler's goal orientation is important for three reasons. One is that goals are constructions the person makes. A goal is a subjective event, and Adler's theory focuses on subjective processes. Secondly, a goal is a cognitive event that represents choice and decision, and Adler's theory focuses on self-determination. In Adler's theory, psychological determination is not based on historical events in a person's life but on the choices and decisions the person makes in setting his course toward future outcomes. Thirdly, the future-orientation of Adler's theory represents the essential optimism inherent in the theory. As a basis for therapy and rehabilitation, the point of view which asserts that behavior is determined by goals is one that indicates the possibility of change: one cannot change history, but one can change one's intentions.

The term *teleological* describes the goal-directed emphasis of Adler's theory. In the 19th century the word "teleological" had a religious meaning, that an ultimate destiny determined a course of events. That is not what Adler meant nor is this a modern conception of the word. The modern use of "teleological" is not mystical, because today the word does not refer to ultimate reality but to the plan or goal that an individual constructs (Wiener, 1948).

A third principle is that humans are above all else *social*. Human actions can be fully understood only in their social significance, and it is this social nature of humans that is the basis for the "need to belong" and for what Adler called *Gemeinschaftsgefühl (Social Interest)*.

In summary, Adler's theory is *holistic, teleological,* and *social*. The many original ideas Adler had, regarding private logic and common sense, inferiority feeling, discouragement and encouragement, family constellation, the tasks of life, to name but a few, all fit congruently with these three basic principles.

CHAPTER 2

SOCIAL INTEREST AND PURPOSIVE BEHAVIOR

When Adler moved away from concern with organ deficiencies and focused primarily on psychological processes, he developed a theory that on the one hand emphasized *subjective* events and on the other hand put great emphasis on *social* events. At a time when many people emphasized biological and physiological determinism and when the major scientific concern was with instinctive processes, Adler's focus on thoughts and ideas, and on social embeddedness, was far ahead of his time.

A goal or an intention is an idea, but it need not be formed at a level of awareness. When a child thinks "I want to go there" the goal specifies the direction in which the child wants to move. As an abstraction of where a person wants to go, a goal is a subjective event that occurs here and now, and is different than an objective event that will happen. The goal is an idea the individual has at a given moment regardless whether the person does or does not reach that outcome. For example, if one has a goal of "I will fight you", this gives direction to the way one behaves, even though a fight may not ensue. It is in this sense that Adler theorized that goals are the basis for motivation and for behavior. Because "I want to go there" does not necessarily refer to a physically concrete place but may refer to a psychological destination, Adlerians stress the importance of understanding a person's "movement". The individual who strives to be the best swimmer, or the richest athlete, or the world's greatest lover, has a goal towards which he or she moves; the goal is clearly identifiable, but it is symbolic rather than concrete in a physical sense of motion.

From the time of infancy, goals give direction for a person's actions. The goal need not be stated verbally, and the person need not be consciously aware of the goal. In the infant the goals are very simple. For example, babies may seek novel or interesting stimulation, they may seek comfort and social stimulation, or socially disturbing infants may seek goals of attention or power.

Because Adler considered that each human is a part of a social community, our sense of self is a function of our social identity. The primary need of all humans is a need to feel belonging, to have a place, in the social community. In the infant, that community is the family. As the person moves into an increasingly larger sphere, the social community to which he or she seeks to feel belonging also becomes increasingly broad. The ultimate social community to which an adult ideally seeks to belong is the human species as a whole, as part of an enlarged sense of one's own humanness. To feel an identity with, and a sense of belonging to, the whole of mankind represents the widest social concern. Some people have a far more restricted view of who is part of their "community." For example, they might include only white persons of a certain income, or only people of a certain nationality. The scope of one's reference group is the way the person defines the social community to which he seeks to belong, and in adulthood this is much more of an abstraction than it is in childhood.

The fundamental "need to belong" binds humans together. What concepts a person has with regard to this need are of major importance. If the child grows up with the conviction that he does belong and has a firm place in the family and, subsequently, in the larger community, his strivings are to contribute to the welfare of the community. The concepts the individual develops regarding his place in society are crucial to the kinds of goals the person develops. The child that is raised in ways that are congruent with Adlerian teachings will "feel himself an equal part of his family" and "an equal part of the whole of mankind" (Adler, 1931/1958, pp. 261-262). However, if the child draws the conclusions that he is not worthy, that he is not good enough as he is and does not have a place, he will direct his energies towards finding a place. Instead of directing his energies towards contribution to human welfare, he will be preoccupied with his own personal status. Thus, the concept the person has regarding whether or not he or she belongs and has a place in society, forms the central basis for the kind of goals the person sets.

Two questions bear on the concept regarding whether or not the person belongs and has a place. One question is: can the conviction that one has a place, that one belongs, ever be attained as a result of one's strivings, or must that conviction first be established, as a given. Dreikurs pointed out that if one doubts that one has a place and belongs, striving to prove that one belongs often results in an unreachable goal. When a person feels that he does not belong and believes that he must prove himself in order to belong, he will strive and *try to find* a place. However, regardless of the successes the person attains, if fundamentally he is convinced he does not belong, his actions are not likely to lead him ever to believe that he has found a place. For this reason, teachers and parents and psychotherapists must help a person know that he "has a place'" and that he "belongs" by his mere existence, not that he has to earn a place or prove that he belongs. The person who believes he has a place can spend his energies on contribution rather than on proving his value or status. The second question is whether striving to contribute is the ideal goal for human beings. Adlerians are unequivocal in answering this affirmatively. As Adler pointed out (Adler, 1931/1958, p.8) "Every human being strives for significance; but people always make mistakes if they do not see that their whole significance must consist in their contribution to the lives of others."

The sense of belonging to the community is what the German word Gemeinschaftsgefühl describes: a feeling ("gefühl") *for* the community ("Gemeinschaft") that also implies a feeling *with*, a sense of oneness with, the community. That is a "feeling" which involves cognition and attitude as well as emotion. It involves concern for the community and its welfare. Adler pointed out that every human being has the innate potential to develop this sense or feeling, and in raising children one can establish the optimum circumstances which lead to the highest development of this feeling. The way the early human contact with the baby is established already sets the social circumstances which either heighten or inhibit the feeling for and with the community. The English translation of Gemeinschaftsgefühl is Social Interest, but that term is misleading if one thinks of interest as merely distant or detached concern. *Identification with the group* is the key to what is called Gemeinschaftsgefühl, and if that is understood by the reader, then Social Interest will not be a misleading term.

In order for the child to identify with the group the child needs to feel a part of the group, to feel that it belongs. The more the child has this feeling the more Social Interest is developed: to belong is not merely a physical or objective fact but a subjective process. That is, a child can know it is a member of a group in an objective sense and still not *feel* a part of it. Such a feeling involves a sense of sharing, of reciprocity, of recognizing that one's membership in the group is important for the group's welfare. Many children grow up knowing that objectively they are members of the family, and in that sense belong, but they believe deeply that they play no significant role in that family and that the family does not need them, that their existence is immaterial to the welfare of the group. In very negative cases, they may even believe the group would be better off without them, that their existence is a hindrance to the welfare of the group.

Out of the feeling of belonging comes the goal of contribution. The feeling of belonging is both a product of, and leads to, a heightened realization of the interdependence of the individual and the group. This in turn leads to contribution and to a concern for the welfare of the whole. Adler pointed out that the potential for Social Interest in every person is innate, but appropriate group processes are required for the innate potential to flower fully. Group processes that involve cooperation, trust, respect for the individual, equality of worth, and that foster shared decision making and sharing of consequences are the kind of processes that most likely will stimulate the growth of Social Interest. Of importance here is not that the group is more vital than the individual but that the individual and group are interdependent. Only when the welfare of each individual in the group is fully considered can the group welfare be maximized; respect for the group cannot supercede respect for the individual. Groups can learn to function increasingly more effectively in this manner, and when the child enters a family that functions in this way the child has the full possibility to develop Social Interest from the earliest age. The group cannot force that development, but it can stimulate it.

At the time Adler put forth his theory there was no apparent analogy for the postulation of an innate potential which requires certain kinds of social experiences for full development. Consequently, his formulation of Social Interest was not easy, for the public and professionals alike, to comprehend. However, recent scientific advancements have brought to light an analogy, and that is language. Humans have the innate capacity to use and understand language, but in order to develop this innate potential they must have appropriate social experiences. Adler's concept of Social Interest can be likened to language: even though humans have the innate potential, neither language nor Social Interest will develop fully without the stimulation provided by appropriate group experiences.

In Adler's theory, Social Interest is the most fundamental process by which the individual can fulfill his or her true human potential. When a person contributes to the welfare of mankind the human being has the possibility to develop his creativity for solving problems, for mastering tasks, for learning and creating, rather than to expend his energies to prove that he is "good enough" or a worthwhile person.

Adlerians have been noted for their concern with how parents raise children and teachers work with students. It should be clear from the above discussion why Adler devoted a great deal of attention to these matters. The younger the person, the more does the individual subjectively assess his or her circumstances on the basis of direct, immediate, objective experiences. Thus, whereas an adult or adolescent may not easily change basic beliefs and goals on the basis of new ways of interaction, when a child experiences positive new social interaction patterns, these new experiences far more readily permit positive goals and attitudes to emerge and grow.

The child comes to have a world view, and a sense of who he or she is and how he or she fits into the larger scheme of things, from early social experiences. Although the child creates his own conclusions based on his experiences and observations, these conclusions are derived from real-life events. The earlier the child experiences harmony and cooperation the more likely that he will build a subjective world view in line with a sense of belonging and a desire to contribute. The child's world view and goals can be more readily molded than can the adult's, thus childhood is the ideal time for the full growth of Social Interest. However, Adlerians point out that Social Interest can be expanded at any age, and indeed, the focus of psychotherapy is to help the client expand his Social Interest.

In summary, the feeling of belonging in the infant and young child helps him develop a self concept that is oriented around self worth, adequacy, competence, and usefulness, and his concept regarding other people will be oriented around trust, decency, and cooperation. The child develops a sense of his identity in the context of group life. The kind of self concept, world view, concept of others, and the goals that the child develops are his own creation, but they reflect the kind of experiences he has. The more he feels he is an important member of the group, the more he recognizes the value of his contribution to group welfare, the more he gains respect for others and from others, the stronger will be his own self confidence as well as his Social Interest. This does not mean an absence of conflict between himself and others nor an absence of discouraging and desparing moments. Rather, it means a readiness to try to find solutions to problems and to learn from life experiences. As he gets older and encounters increasingly more social contacts and expands his memberships in groups, he will build on a solid foundation: one that gives maximum opportunity for positive human relationships, for living a creative and productive life, and for the courage to master difficulties and to cope with defeats.

CHAPTER 3

COURAGE, INFERIORITY FEELING, and SUPERIORITY STRIVING

Adlerians have observed that Social Interest helps "other people" and society. Still, one could ask "Why is Social Interest of great value for the individual personally?" Although there are many ways to answer this question, one word — "courage" — fits all the answers. When a person has the conviction that he or she belongs to the human community and has a life goal of contributing to the human community, the individual is not worried about personal prestige and not fearful about his or her value as a human being. Such worries and fears, which sap enormous amounts of energy, beset many people. Adlerians have found this to occur when people do not have a large amount of Social Interest. Preoccupation with self and one's value is not likely to be productive. In contrast, a concern with contribution brings strength instead of cost to the person. Social Interest helps to bring courage in many ways: it provides courage to try new things, to solve problems, to interact with people, to work cooperatively with others, and to focus on the task at hand rather than on side issues. Problem solving and task orientation replace preoccupation with one's prestige. Consequently, when one has Social Interest, one is more likely to function effectively. In difficult situations, one is likely to assess the circumstances and identify how one can improve performance, rather than to intepret inadequate performance as a sign of personal failing and defeat. Social Interest helps the individual separate the *deed* from the *doer:* one realizes that mistakes are inevitable, and that they do not imply the person is a failure. Social Interest provides courage and helps a person "not to give up" but to "try again" to deal with obstacles and setbacks.

Self-confidence is a by-product of Social Interest. When one contributes to other's well-being, this reinforces and increases the sense of one's own strength; and when one is discouraged about difficulties and problems in life, Social Interest leads to those kinds of behaviors that are most likely to heighten self-confidence. The pattern is circular. If initially one is sure of one's place, this belief leads to self-confidence and Social Interest: yet, if one later encounters discouraging experiences and thereby loses self-confidence, Social Interest will help the person to function more effectively and to cope better with the difficulties, and this in turn will help restore self-confidence. What is here meant by self-confidence is the belief "I can do it" or "I can cope." That is different from "I have a place, I belong." Since other kinds of motivations can lead to self-confidence, it is necessary to consider the unique role of Social Interest. For example, research has shown that children and adults with a high achievement motive (McClelland, 1958, 1962, 1973) are more self-confident and more willing to take realistic risks than are persons with a low achievement motive (also called the "need to achieve"). High achievement motivated persons tend to be more optimistic, and they are more concerned with seeking success than with avoiding failure. They are more self-reliant and task oriented than persons with a low achievement motive. In these ways high achievement motivation leads to comparable behaviors and attitudes as the motivation to contribute. However, persons with a high "need to achieve" are primarily concerned with attaining success by means of their own efforts, and therefore such persons are not necessarily effective in situations that call for cooperation and group problem solving. The important point to note is that self-confidence per se is not sufficient to meet the problems of living, to provide courage in a wide variety of situations, and to bring flexible coping strategies.

If one is concerned only with one's own accomplishments, without a concommitant concern for others and for a value system that requires contribution to the welfare of others, then one may find oneself limited in the extent to which one lives harmoniously with others. Ordinarily, contribution involves accomplishing tasks and performing skillfully. Even simple tasks can be done well or shoddily, and high levels of achievement can lead to great contributions to society. However, an exclusive preoccupation with one's own achievements is likely to lead to barriers for working well with others. If one is concerned only with one's own achievements it is often difficult to recognize the needs of others or the "needs of the situation." Many persons who are "successful" in business or the professions have a large amount of self-confidence and can achieve great accomplishments, yet they are perplexed why their marriages are not successful and their children fail to measure up to their potential. A lack of concern for others' welfare limits one's interpersonal skills and understanding, so that self-confidence, as a conviction of "I can do it", is not enough for effective living.

Social Interest provides a perspective which enables the person to function with courage in a wide variety of situations and tasks. When one is not concerned with defending or proving one's status, one is able to appreciate many aspects of life and to learn from many experiences. Cooperation occurs not only with other persons but with life, in general. Social Interest does not guarantee success in life nor does it guarantee that all obstacles can be overcome well. However, to the extent that courage is required for effective living, to that extent the most consistent courage results from Social Interest. It is not the courage involved in great physical feats or daring actions, but the courage of meeting the continuing challenges of a lifetime.

Social Interest is sometimes mistaken with other motivations, such as striving to please others or striving to conform. Because contribution often requires creative approaches rather than conformity, and because conformity may actually hamper helping others, conformity is not at all what is meant by Social Interest. Likewise, pleasing others is not the same as Social Interest, even though often when one contributes this does please others. The difference is in the intent. If the person strives to please rather than primarily to contribute, the person is likely to strive to please even when that is antithetical to contribution. One often has to be willing to incur other people's displeasure in order to contribute. A parent who "cannot stand" to say "no" to his or her child because of the desire to please, is often not contributing to the child's welfare. The goal is not contribution but personal gains. Pleasing others, as a means of making oneself liked, is different than helping to solve a problem or improving a situation. When one pleases others as a by-product of contribution, it is not the same as pleasing others as a means of enhancing one's own status.

The courage to say "no" which stems from the striving to contribute can be sometimes mistakenly attributed to defiance or rebellion that is directed towards the goal of attention or of power. Just as conformity is not the same as Social Interest, so is anti-conformity not the same as Social Interest. Even though many rebels use arguments that sound like concern for the common good, the goal of contribution can be distinguished by the degree to which the person seeks solutions rather than special status, and by the degree to which the person pursues cooperation rather than conflict.

Striving to contribute differs from striving for prestige or special status. Then why, if contribution is so valuable to the individual and to society, would a person strive to gain attention or power or prestige? From an Adlerian point of view, persons strive for specialness or superiority in order to overcome feelings of inadequacy and inferiority. When an individual does not feel belonging, the person believes he or she is "not good enough" and feels inferior. This feeling is with regard to one's status and value as a human being. As a result of adverse training in childhood, many people grow up with the conviction that they are not adequate and that they are inferior. In the second period of his writing, Adler said that since the baby is born into a world of bigger and stronger people, it will conclude it is inferior. However, in the later, third, period of his theoretical formulations, Adler recognized that if children were raised with cooperation and equality instead of competitiveness and vertical strivings, inferiority feelings would not be inevitable and universal. Instead, children would feel belonging and assured of having a place and being of value. Inferiority feeling thus represents a mistaken "feeling" that results from discouraging experiences.

Adler pointed out that two kinds of childhood experiences are especially likely to lead to inferiority feelings. One is being pampered and babied, with the child not doing things for himself, and other people over-protecting and "spoiling" the child. The other case is the rejected and neglected child, with the child being treated as an outcast and not receiving the care it needs. The first type of situation leads to feelings of inferiority because the child is denied experiences which permit him to contribute and realize his own strength. He or she grows up convinced that others must take care of him or her. Such a child feels unable to contribute and has a low sense of self-confidence. The neglected child also does not feel able to contribute since others do not welcome contribution and reject his efforts. Discouragement is evident in both kinds of children.

To overcome feeling inferior, the child tries to find his or her place by a variety of means. Most frequently these involve goals of attention or power. If the child does not feel an equal, he or she will try to find a place by being *special* in some way. This may be by useful means, such as being a diligent student or good athlete or doing heroic deeds, or it may be by disturbing or destructive means, such as being a show-off or a bully or a vandal. Within this vertical process, the child mistakes superiority with equality. In striving to overcome feeling inferior, the child is likely to strive to be superior in the mistaken belief that he or she will then be "special like the others" and thus their equal. The child is not aware that he pursues a goal of being special as a way of overcoming his feeling of inferiority. However, using proper methods of disclosure in a counseling situation, the counselor without difficulty can help the young child to recognize his mistaken beliefs and goals. With older children and adults such disclosure is more difficult, since more entrenched beliefs (convictions) and goals exist in older children and adults.

Dreikurs (1947, 1948, 1957) described the four mistaken goals of children who do not feel they belong and whose goal is not that of contribution. These four goals refer to the child's trying to find a "special" place, in his mistaken belief that this might bring "belonging." First is the goal of attention. The child mistakenly concludes "only if I gain attention am I of value, only then do I belong." The goal of attention may be directed in useful ways, such as being a special helper to the teacher or being "the good child" at home. Attention may also be directed in ways that are "useless", in the sense that they do not add positively to either the individual's or others' lives. The child who bothers his or her classmates, who teases his or her siblings, who spills and is sloppy or clumsy, gains attention in ways that disturb others. Dreikurs has described this goal in many of his books. For example, when the child seeks attention by annoying he will stop his behavior, but only temporarily, with reprimand. Moreover, "pleasing" behavior will possibly turn to annoying behavior if attention is not gained for "useful" acts. Attention as a goal can be easily distinguished from contribution because contribution continues whether or not the person receives attention.

Children who strive to be special and who feel discouraged about finding a place by means of attention are likely to turn to another goal, that of power. The goal of power can take many forms but they always signify domination. A child or adult with a goal of power may be a bully or overt tyrant but also may display more subtle forms of tyranny. The child can use "weakness" as well as strength to be a tyrant. The child who dominates others by his fears or his sicknesses can gain as much power over others as can the bully who fights and screams. The goal of domination reflects the sentiment of "You must do what I want" and is therefore more disturbing than the goal of attention. It also reflects a more discouraged outlook on the child's part. In reference to disturbing behavior, the distinction is between mastery over people versus mastery over tasks. A goal of power does not refer to the child who wants his own way in solving problems or accomplishing tasks, if in this process he does not also seek to dominate other persons. Power refers to interpersonal domination, and by denying respect to others the power-oriented person, whether child or adult, disturbs harmony and cooperation.

If the discouraged child concludes that through power he cannot find a place, and he feels himself deeply hurt, he may seek a third goal, that of revenge. As the child feels increasingly discouraged and hurt, he will try to find his place with decreasing amounts of Social Interest. A goal of superiority in which he seeks to hurt others as he himself feels hurt may be the only way the child believes he can find some kind of status. The goal of revenge, in which the child seeks to retaliate and hurt others, represents a great deal of discouragement on the part of the child. He or she no longer believes that he or she is accepted and wanted, and so the child adopts extreme measures of asserting his or her importance. If even this approach to life fails, and the child is even more discouraged and becomes convinced he cannot gain any significance at all, he may adopt the fourth goal. That is a goal of complete withdrawal and characterizes the condition Adler called "inferiority complex." The child with such a goal no longer makes outward efforts to establish a superior status. The goal of specialness is one of "leave me alone." The child with this goal no longer believes that any effort will help. If adults attempt to be helpful, by his reactions he will be able to discourage the adults themselves, to such a point that they also believe there is no hope for the child. The reader who seeks to understand these four goals far more thoroughly will find valuable information in books by Dreikurs, Grunwald, and Pepper (1971/1982) and Dreikurs and Soltz (1964).

Adults adopt more complex forms of superiority strivings, but like the child, they may strive by "useful" or "useless" means. They may try to find a place by superiority strivings that benefit society or their impact may have no benefit. Because by adulthood the person has a Life Style that permits a variety of actions and short-term goals, the adult does not display the clearly identifiable four mistaken goals described for the child.

Adler viewed all problems of maladjustment as deficiencies in Social Interest. Neurosis, psychosis, delinquency, as well as many psychological disorders, reflect a person's striving for special status based on deep inferiority feelings. Helping the person to re-direct his goals and beliefs, towards removal of interiority feeling and toward increased feeling of belonging and Social Interest, is thus the aim of all Adlerian counseling, psychotherapy, and education.

CHAPTER 4

PRIVATE LOGIC, COMMON SENSE, AND LIFE STYLE

Adlerians put emphasis on subjective rather than objective "causality," believing that an individual's actions are not based directly on objective circumstances but on the person's interpretation of them. Adlerians seek to understand the "private logic" of each person and to identify the individual's apperceptions.

The word "apperception," used by non-Adlerians like Henry Murray (1938), is a useful term. When an individual looks at objects or scenes, especially ambiguous ones that are not sharply defined or that have a somewhat fuzzy appearance, two processes are likely to occur. The person *perceives* the objects or scenes, in ways that are physiologically determined by the visual pathways, and the person *interprets* what he or she perceives, on the basis of goals, expectations, emotions, and other non-visual processes. The interpretation of perceived events is *apperception*. The process of apperception occurs in many circumstances, especially in interpersonal situations. Individuals typically do not only *perceive* the events, but add interpretation to the visual and auditory information. The process of interpretation is very rapid and usually occurs without the person's awareness, so that the individual believes he "saw" events in a certain fashion without realizing how much additional meaning he added to the visual input. In addition to interpreting what is perceived, individuals also selectively attend to and selectively remember what is perceived. Thus in a variety of ways, information regarding objective events is structured and often modified by ، tive, subjective processes. This occurs normally in everyday life, and psychologists in general, not only Adlerians, are beginning to study systematically how this occurs in the normal process of seeing, remembering, and interpreting perceptual events. Although psychologists in general are increasingly focusing on the way the individual organizes and modifies his perceptions, it is useful to note in the present context that from the start Adler's theory emphasized the importance of subjective processes in a person's actions and in the way the individual assesses (apperceives) the events around him.

Adler was a pioneer in many ways. One was that he emphasized the importance of subjective processes in the development of personality. Although Freud is properly credited as the person who initially emphasized that personality affects everyday thought, fantasy, action, and emotion, Freud nevertheless considered that the formation of personality was determined by objective circumstances in childhood. In contrast, Adler stated that from infancy on, the human being forms his reactions and creates his experiences, and that through his interpretations, actions, and goals, the child shapes his personality. Adler pointed out that early family life sets the stage for personality development, but each individual child in the family creates his or her own interpretations and goals, and from these creates the individual *Life Style*. Thus, within the framework of each person's heredity and objective environment, the individual in childhood develops a pattern and a scheme for ways to live, to adapt, to grow, and to meet life's problems and opportunities. This pattern and scheme is developed through a creative process, on the basis of subjective appraisal and individual decision making.

According to Adler, from birth on each child actively integrates his experiences, and he does this in his own individual fashion. The child already in infancy develops simple plans and goals. In this respect, Adler's theory is congruent with Piaget's formulations of the growth of intellect (Piaget, 1953, 1955), which stated that the young child develops simple schemas that provide a basis for perception and action. However, in other respects Adler's theory differed from that of Piaget. Adler emphasized goals, and in Adler's theory but not in Piaget's the importance of goals and schemas lay in their social and psychodynamic nature.

Adler found that the behavior of even young infants shows direction and pattern, and by the end of the first year of life purposive behavior and patterned striving can be very clearly identified. Increasingly, the child's assessments of immediate circumstances become integrated into a "view of life." This is at first tentative but it becomes molded, by trial and error methods, into a coherent set of concepts. The subjective schemas represent a *private logic* which makes sense to the child even if the adults consider the schemas invalid and "illogical." By the time the child is around five or six years old his hypotheses about the meaning of life have been tested many times, and he comes to believe that his beliefs are true. The child does not recognize the subjectivity of his beliefs and considers them objectively valid. Thus, Adler said by the time the child is around five or six years old he has developed a *Life Style*, which is a mode of relating to the world: it contains a basic self concept and life goal, a world view, and a fundamental mode of dealing with life situations *(modus operandi)* which remains relatively stable over the individual's life time.

Life Style remains relatively stable because, in accepting his basic beliefs and life pattern as truths, the individual interprets new life events in line with his prior convictions rather than altering his convictions in the face of new experiences. Moreover, since the individual selects friends and experiences in line with his life goals and beliefs, he is not likely to encounter drastically contrary new information about himself and others. To the extent that parents, teachers, and counselors can understand the child's private logic and help provide alternative and positive life experiences that widen the child's Social Interest and give him more encouragement, to that extent is the child likely to modify his Life Style beyond the age of six years. However, if such alternatives do not occur in the elementary school age years, the child will come to adopt a firmly set life goal and world view which leads to a Life Style that under ordinary circumstances is not modified except through psychotherapy.

Private logic within Adlerian theory pertains to both adults' and children's concepts, for individual bias is part of human understanding and motivation. The biased nature of thought is often not noticed nor a source of difficulty, since in much of everyday living human communication is based on shared meaning and consensus. Beliefs and the meaning of words are typically agreed on by members of a culture, and *common sense* provides the norm for much of human action. Although Adler pointed out that individuals interpret events in terms of their unique apperceptions, Adler also emphasized the importance of common sense for society and for human action.

Contrary to Freud's formulation of a divided self (ego, superego, and id), Adler did not say that individuals have internal conflict between their private logic and their common sense. Rather, a person's behavior follows individual goals and beliefs as well as the communal process. In psychosis the private logic can deviate from the common sense to an extreme degree. However, individuals with psychosis do not necessarily show this deviation under all circumstances or in all situations. Dreikurs often remarked that a psychotic person may show a great deal of community feeling and common sense in situations within which the person feels belonging and encouraged, even though in other situations the person may experience delusions and hallucinations.

Life Style, as the core of personality, provides and represents unity, individuality, coherence, and stability of a person's psychological functioning. The long-term life goal of the individual and the fundamental self-concept and world view of each person provide a blueprint that gives character and structure to the way the individual lives. Choices of friends and careers, of whom to love and to marry, are all congruent with the basic goal and concepts of the Life Style. The variety of behavior that is shown by each person throughout the course of his life reflects the person's varied immediate goals which occur as the individual encounters many circumstances over the course of a life span. The short-term or immediate goals are always congruent with the long-term goal of the Life Style, but within a given Life Style a wide range of short-term goals are possible. Moreover, if the Life Style is based on Social Interest and the individual has a broadly-based world view and self-concept, the more varied and creative are the short-term goals likely to be. Adlerians have developed certain techniques which permit the therapist or counselor to understand a person's Life Style. Dreikurs considered that Early Recollections and information regarding the individual's Family Constellation are basic to understanding Life Style. (Some of Dreikurs' views were described by Ferguson, 1964). Other techniques, such as dream interpretation, art therapy, and psychodrama, provide very useful diagnostic information. Although these latter techniques are more likely to reveal short-term goals rather than the long-term goal of the Life Style, under the guidance of skilled Adlerians these techniques have been found to be extremely valuable. For example, the family constellation may be depicted in psychodrama and individuals may act out Early Recollections.

It is useful to distinguish between short-term and long-term goals. For many persons who seek psychological help, a major change in the Life Style may not be necessary. Rather, a change in only certain immediate goals may help to remove difficulties and to improve effective living. Nevertheless, the understanding of Life Style, regardless of whether or not the person wishes to change it, is often immensely valuable as a means for understanding the pattern of one's apperceptions, actions, and decisions.

Many persons initially find these general principles difficult to apply in everyday life. Within our culture we do not learn to understand goals or private logic. Thus we need illustrations to translate Adler's ideas into practical living. For example, many persons recognize that their actions "don't make sense." People often say "I know better than that. Why did I behave this way?" These comments reflect that the person is aware of the common sense, but, additionally, that the person fails to recognize his private logic. Children and adults often know what they should do or what the rules are and yet the person behaves in a very different way. From an Adlerian point of view it is not a case of ambivalence or a lack of will power, but rather that each person behaves in line with his goal. If the goal is "I want to be boss" or "no one is going to tell me what to do", then doing what one is supposed to do or what is "good for you" may seem like defeat. Giving in to common sense, from the private logic of the person, is submission. Behaving in ways that are contrary to what one "should" do may be a way of showing who is boss: "I can do whatever I please — others can behave sensibly if they feel like it, but I'm going to do what I please." And so, in line with the person's private logic, he or she eats too much, drinks too much, or has too many love affairs — where "too much" is judged in terms of common sense which the person, by choice, defies according to his private logic. Only when the person's goal is changed, when the person no longer wants to be boss and no longer thinks "to hell with you, all of you, I'll do what I want", will the person's action fall in line with common sense. As our goals become directed towards contribution, as we feel more belonging and seek more to meet task demands, so also will our actions move in line with common sense. In some cases, this may require only a change in short-term goals. In other cases, this will require a major change in Life Style. Since short-term goals are never contrary to the persons's Life Style, a change in Life Style may be necessary for the person to behave more in accord with common sense.

CHAPTER 5

FAMILY CONSTELLATION AND SIBLING RELATIONSHIPS

Because in Adler's theory the individual's personality is formed in the first few years of life, the early years are crucial for the well-being of the child and, subsequently, for the person in adulthood. Parent education is thus vital, since future difficulties can be prevented when parents learn to raise their children in line with Adlerian principles.

In the early years of family life the child develops his basic concepts of self and of life in general. Through his family interactions the child first experiences cooperation or conflict, encouragement or discouragement, equality of worth or inferiority feeling. He discovers the degree to which he can participate and share, to trust and be trusted, and he develops concepts of possible alliances or competition.

Contrary to Freud, Adler emphasized the whole family, in its total structure and dynamic interactions. Freud considered only the mother-child and father-child relationships to be significant for the child's personality development, with resolution of the Oedipus complex (for boys) and Electra complex (for girls) involving all three persons. Freud did not consider the siblings important. However, for Adler the sibling relationships were very important. Adler is well known for his emphasis on birth order, for recognizing that each child in the family has a unique *ordinal position* which shapes his or her own, unique, perspective. All family members make up a social unit and objectively they live in the same family. However, the social environment of significant "others" is different for each member of the family, and each member of the family has unique experiences and interactions. Each person draws subjective conclusions and forms individual apperceptions that are not necessarily shared by other members of the family.

Although Adler is well known for emphasizing birth order, his views on this are often misunderstood. The position of the child in the birth order provides only probabilities, not certainty, that the child will have specific types of experiences. It is likely, but not certain, that first-born children will be dominant types of individuals and youngest children will be charmers. This is because in our culture the birth order in most families tends to lead to different types of inter-relationships for oldest, middle, and youngest children. Although Adlerians have identified birth order as a significant factor in the child's personality development, a given type of behavior pattern cannot be predicted on the basis of birth order alone. Not only does a culture and its norms change, but a specific family may have atypical interactions among its members. Ordinal position is thus dynamically significant but does not in itself predict a fixed personality type.

The family is a dynamic whole. The birth of each child brings a new member into the family group, and with it the emergence of new interaction patterns. Each newcomer enters a group that has existing patterns, but after arriving the newcomer also adds his or her own contributions. Structural factors, like birth order, make specific patterns of apperception and interaction more likely, such as first-borns receiving special attention and high parental standards which may not be received by later born children. In the final analysis, however, what matters is the family dynamics as a whole. Adler's holism pertains equally to family dynamics, and to group dynamics in general, as it does to individual dynamics. Ordinal position describes one important aspect of family structure, and as such it helps to shape each child's apperceptions and the interaction patterns that occur between the family members.

In many families the first-born strives to assert his or her dominance and bosses the younger siblings, while the youngest child in the family strives to find a place by being charming. Being the last born, sometimes the youngest child is very ambitious and strives for high achievement in his effort to overtake and outdo the older siblings. Many middle children feel squeezed and have a world view that life is unfair. Often the middle child strives to find his place by being an arbitrator concerned with justice. In this way, birth order may predict specific apperceptions, goals, and personality characteristics. However, the patterns in any given family will differ somewhat from the cultural norm. For example, in some families the oldest girl may be constantly discouraged and belittled while a later-born male child is given wide rein. To assess the personality development of each child in the family, it is not sufficient to know the person's ordinal position. A full understanding of the family dynamics and of the "movement" of each person in the family is required.

Adler recognized that children in the family shape their personality development in terms of the ways each tries to find a place in the group. As the child "moves" to find a place, he develops behavior tendencies that shape his personality on the basis of the total interaction patterns of the family. The child develops those attributes and characteristics that he or she believes will help him or her find a place. If a family has strong competition and does not provide encouragement nor emphasizes Social Interest and equality of worth, the children are likely to develop a competitive pattern, which becomes manifest in their developing opposite personality characteristics. Dreikurs summarized it best in his *Fundamentals of Adlerian Psychology* (Dreikurs, 1950, p.40):

> As each member of the family strives for his own place within the group, the competing opponents watch each other carefully to see the ways and means by which the opponent succeeds or fails. Where one succeeds, the other gives up; where one shows weakness or deficiencies, the other steps in. In this way competition between two members of the family is always expressed through differences in character, temperament, interests, and abilities. Conversely, the similarity of characteristics always indicates alliances. Sometimes, the two strongest competitors show no sign of open rivalry but, rather, present a close-knit pair; nevertheless, their competitive striving is expressed in personality differences.

Thus, similarities and differences in temperament and behavior are formed in the early years as movements in a dynamic, interpersonal, process. Sibling relationships reflect alliance or competition with respect to finding a place in the family. If the children do not believe that they each have a place or that all of them can find a place, they will strive competitively, at each other's expense, to try to find a place. They will believe they have to fight for a place and will push one another down in competitive striving. The glory of one will be the defeat of the other one, in a see-saw pattern that finds no winners. Sometimes two or more siblings will form alliances against one or more common "enemy". In such an alliance the siblings' strivings will lead to similarities rather than to see-saw, opposite, qualities. Not only siblings but parents and children can form alliances and competition, such as, for example, mother and youngest child against father and oldest child.

Many times the first-born child interprets the birth of the second child as a threat to his status. Adler aptly spoke of this as "dethronement," which describes what happens when a royal prince is born who literally can dethrone the first-born. That type of event has occurred many times in history when the first-born is a girl and the second child is a boy and the royal line is based on a masculine hierarchy. Whether or not it is the fear of dethronement, the most frequent relationship between the first and second child is that of competition (Ferguson, 1958), with the two children developing opposite personality characteristics. Usually the first and third child form an alliance against the second, although a wide range of possibilities exists. Even identical twins can be competitors and develop opposite personalities.

The age difference between children in the family and the sex of the siblings each plays a role in the *family constellation*. The family constellation defines the "characters in the drama" of the early formative years of each person. A full description of the family constellation includes the sex and ages of all the family members that were living in the child's home in his or her formative years. This may have included grandparents, aunts and uncles, and any other persons who were integrated into the household and lived with the child. A review of the family constellation will include lines of interaction, such as which persons imitated and which persons rebelled against one another, who supported and who opposed each other and in which ways. The family values also are significant. In a family that valued intellect, the rebel would develop non-intellectual modes of action; in a family that valued athletics, the rebel might strive to be an intellect.

Because the Life Style develops within the given family constellation, in order to understand the adult it is important that information regarding the family constellation of the person's childhood is re-created retrospectively. Adler pointed out that since the Life Style involves movement toward a goal that the person set for himself in childhood, the meaning of that goal can only be grasped by understanding the context in which it was formulated. Thus, for example, a goal of wanting "to be outstanding, to be out in front, a real man" (Ferguson, 1964, p.411) would have a very different meaning if the man were the oldest child with four younger brothers whom he strove to outpace, than if the man were the youngest child with no brothers and four older sisters who spoiled and pampered him.

The family as a whole, in its total pattern of interactions, provides the field for the child's early life experiences. Because certain objective experiences have a greater likelihood of leading to Social Interest, courage, and alliance among members of the whole family, the subjective assessment and goal of each individual is not independent of the early childhood experiences. The fact that each Life Style develops in a creative and unique way does not mean the objective field of experiences is irrelevant. Rather, the child often correctly observes events but gives them erroneous interpretations.

By means of psychotherapy, the adult can learn to have a new understanding of his early formative years and he can re-direct his beliefs and goals. The "truths" of his childhood can be replaced and alternative modes of behavior can be followed. With respect to parent education, it is important that parents learn to understand the child's private logic as well as to provide cooperative family experiences that facilitate the development of a feeling of belonging and a goal of contribution. The parents play a significant role in setting the atmosphere in the household, in providing the family values, in showing how conflicts can be resolved and in defining the rules of social living. Parents can learn to understand the child's goals and the way the child develops his personality in a social context. From an awareness of the family patterns, both parents and children can work toward optimum patterns of functioning as individuals and as a family.

CHAPTER 6

EARLY RECOLLECTIONS, THE PSYCHOLOGY OF USE, CONSCIOUS, AND UNCONSCIOUS

The formative years of early childhood are important in Adler's theory because they shape goals and attitudes that last a lifetime. The apperceptions and interpretations rather than the objective facts by themselves leave a lasting mark on the personality of the child and subsequently on the adult. Subjective aspects are crucial for development, and they are important in the way the person in adulthood recalls his early childhood.

Early Recollections are crucial for identifying the person's Life Style because they represent the movement and life concepts of the adult who recalls the specific childhood events. Early Recollections have a special meaning in Adler's theory. They are specific incidents that occurred before the age of 8, which the person can identify concretely as an occurrence. Dreikurs distinguished between an Early Recollection and a report. By a report Dreikurs meant either a set of events that lacked a concrete beginning and end, and which the person indicates as having happened many times, or an event that the person does not recall but assumes happened because others told of the occurrence.*

An Early Recollection is an encapsulated, specific event with a beginning and end. The adult in telling it can usually identify a scene, with highlights, and with clear recall of how the person felt in the scene. Early Recollections form a projective technique in Adlerian psychology (Ferguson, 1964; Mosak, 1958). Adlerians assume that the person chooses to recall those events from childhood which fortify his basic goal and convictions about himself and the world (Adler, 1931/1958). In other words, the person recalls events clearly and sharply as a means of giving justification to his basic goal and beliefs, as a means of maintaining his Life Style.

An example can be given of a person who believes that life is unfair and untrustworthy and that the person himself is a victim of other people's machinations and failings; the person's goal (and the only one he believes to be possible) is to look down on others and to show how unfair they are, since he is convinced that, otherwise, people will always take advantage of him. A person with such a Life Style cannot readily maintain these beliefs with a set of memories that depict him as an effective child among other people who are kind and helpful to him. However, memories that reveal the untrustworthiness of other persons and the entrapment of the person when he was a child, would give full support to the adult's conviction and basic life goal. Through the specific Early Recollections the individual tells himself and others: "This is the way the world is and this is my lot in life; this is the only solution for me." What is important for Adlerians is not that the events ever really

---

* Some Adlerians accept such "told" occurrences as reflecting Life Style, although for Dreikurs these "told" events were not as valid for revealing Life Style as were Early Recollections. (See Ferguson (1964) for a fuller description of the procedure.) Also, some Adlerian psychotherapists have found it helpful to get persons to "make up" an Early Recollection, since also such constructions have been found to represent selection and choices that fit in with the Life Style. However, this is not a typical procedure for collecting and studying Early Recollections.

happened but that the person believes the events happened, that the person believes those are factual and true historic occurrences.

The Early Recollections form a pattern and a theme. The Adlerian-trained psychotherapist recognizes the movement in the recollections and the way the recollections form a pattern to depict "This is the story of my life." Whether the person in childhood would have reported the event, whether ten years earlier the adult would have recalled exactly the same details, are no more crucial than whether the event ever really occurred. What does matter is the constancy of the goal and basic concepts. Adlerians believe that Early Recollections told by the person at an earlier age would have revealed the same goal and concepts. Adler maintained that a person's Life Style is stable over many years; a person might give different events in his Early Recollections at another time, but Adlerians would predict that the same life goal and basic concepts would be manifested.

This assumption, that we selectively remember in line with our goals, is fundamental for Adlerians. We choose to select out of the *current* and *present* circumstances those aspects that fit our *immediate goals;* if we demand that everyone in the room should admire us, we shall notice the one person who frowns or looks disinterested. We select those aspects of the situation that fit our immediate purpose. Adler's is a "psychology of use"; we select that which is useful to us, that fits our purpose (goal). In the same way, Early Recollections are ours by selection; they are our use of the *past* to fit our *long-range purpose*. The mood, the specific encapsulated scene, of the Early Recollection in its vividness is our selection of what is crucial about life. As the Life Style is changed with psychotherapy, so also does the message of the Early Recollections change. In some cases, the whole content is forgotten, while in other cases only some parts are forgotten and new parts are remembered for the first time. Dreikurs used to say that the extent to which the Early Recollections change over the course of psychotherapy represents a key indication of the extent to which the Life Style has changed.

The "psychology of use" does not mean that we are aware of the fact that we recall events which serve our purpose. People are not aware of their long-term goals and often are not aware of more immediate goals, and in recalling childhood events, a person is not aware of *why* specific events are recalled. The person assumes that the recalled events are objectively true and therefore are vivid. The person is not aware he selects the events, and he or she cannot envision the possibility that the events might never have even occurred.

We behave in certain ways in line with our purpose, but we need not be conscious of our purpose nor of the way our behavior fits the purpose. Adler defined "conscious" as "aware" and "unconscious" as "unaware", and at different times we can be aware or unaware of a given goal or behavior. In Adler's theory, "conscious" and "unconscious" are relative, not absolute nor crucially distinct. For Freud "unconscious" had very special meaning, and in fact it was capitalized and given a place in the structure of personality, "the Unconscious." In contrast, Adler gave no special status to unconscious as opposed to conscious processes. We are aware or unaware of our actions and purposes according to what has value or use at a given time. If awareness of the purpose of our actions will help us execute our actions more effectively, then we are more likely to be aware (conscious) of them. Alternatively, if knowing the purpose of our actions is not going to help us, or if it even will prevent us from being more effective in attaining our goal, then we are likely *not* to be conscious of the purpose.

The importance given to unconscious processes in some theories, like those of Freud and Jung, stems from the assumption in those theories that "the Unconscious" has some kind of dynamic force of its own, that unconscious processes "make" a person do things. In Adler's theory each person is a decision maker who determines his own actions, and unconscious forces do not "make us do things." Thus, a strong distinction between unconscious and conscious processes is not necessary within Adler's theory.

The psychology of use does not assume a hedonic principle, that we do those things that give us pleasure. Rather, we do things that are "logical" and make sense, either in terms of private logic or in terms of common sense, but in any case that our actions and goals have some kind of rationale. The psychology of use has sometimes been attacked as overly pragmatic or materialistic, and Adler has been accused of wrongly assuming that people behave as if they were economists. Opponents of Adler's theory cite the prevalence of "irrationality", that human action is often self-defeating and irrational. However, when Adler proposed his psychology of use he did not suggest that "irrational" behavior won't occur. Rather, one must spell out the frame of reference of "whose rationality" is under consideration. Some persons in their private logic make incredible assumptions about themselves and life. By standards of common sense their beliefs are irrational. But from the viewpoint of the person himself, his beliefs and actions follow his logic and subjective sense. Thus, even though from others' point of view an act may be "senseless", each person pursues goals and actions which are useful in terms of that person's assessment of circumstances. "Usefulness" does not mean one is conscious or aware of one's subjective beliefs nor that one understands why one pursues certain goals. However, when through counseling, an individual's private logic is disclosed, the "usefulness" of the individual's actions will be readily apparent. For example, a woman who wishes to avoid commitments of marriage may wonder why she is always attracted to married men and falls in love only with men who are already otherwise attached. She might blame unconscious urges she cannot control. She might complain at her bad fortune or her irrationality. However, although she's not aware of this, from the point of view of her own subjective perspective, it is far more useful for her to have love affairs with persons that offer no prospect of marriage. In a counseling situation this can be discussed, and once the person is aware of the purpose of her action, she may or may not decide to continue the same kind of actions in the future. She may decide it is in her best interest to avoid the commitment of marriage, and she may thus consciously continue her former actions. With awareness she recognizes that she has a choice and that her actions follow her own decision making.

Since subjectivity is a part of psychological life, we are not aware of many of our actions or goals.* We often need an external perspective in order to be aware of our own goals and beliefs. Awareness can be extremely helpful. If we know what we are doing and for what purpose, it is easier to evaluate our actions and goals, and it is then far easier to make new choices and decisions. But in many cases, awareness only interferes with smooth movement and efficient functioning. For example, if we are aware of how we talk and how we walk, our attention is likely to switch to motor

---

* Dreikurs (1963) spoke of the "psychological uncertainty principle", that we either are in action, that is, in the process of moving toward a goal, or we analyze and reflect on that action, but we cannot be both observer and actor at the same identical moment.

acts which are far more efficient without such attention. The same can occur in our dealings with other people. Awareness might disrupt the smooth flow of our interpersonal relationships; awareness may lead to hesitancy and awkwardness which interfere with previously smooth patterns of social interactions. For Adlerians, "aware" and "unaware" are fluid states, that vary with circumstances and according to the "logic" of the individual who is making choices and decisions. Because most people have not learned to recognize goals and private logic, much of their awareness focuses on other aspects of their lives. However, awareness can be increased through training in Adlerian methods and theory.

CHAPTER 7

EMOTIONS, CONSCIENCE, AND GUILT FEELINGS

Emotions can be said to provide fuel for action, and in Adler's theory, emotions always serve a purpose. Our varied emotions (such as being sad, happy, angry, or loving) "move" us in a direction, not just away from something, but toward some goal. For example, a child who is sad and sulking may be seeking pity or help from another child or adult. A person who feels love and happiness may be seeking intimacy and love from another person. When we are angry we often intimidate another person and get what we want from the other one.

An illustration can be given with a family that had two sons, aged 10 and 12 years. The younger boy, struggling to defeat the older brother, had succeeded for many years: the younger was better looking, was an excellent swimmer, was highly successful academically as well as athletically, and in every possible way, he was a wonderful boy with a fine disposition and no problems. The older boy, as can be expected from Adler's concept of sibling competition, was completely discouraged: he did not do well in school work nor in athletics, was bad tempered, had very few friends, was rarely happy, and was mostly glum or sad or angry. The family sought help, and in Adlerian fashion, the whole family was asked to come for counseling. Both children were counseled, and also the parents, to help the first child feel more confident. Adlerians who understand sibling competition know that once the "bad" child improves, it is very possible that the formerly "good" child can become very discouraged and change drastically in actions and emotions. That is what happened in this family. A deep competition existed in the family, between the brothers and between the two parents, with each looking to see "if you are successful, I cannot be; and if I am successful, you cannot be." Thus, as the older son gained more courage and belief in himself, the younger one "gave up". Within a short time he had problems in school and his grades dropped; whereas he was an excellent swimmer, he suddenly did not want to swim anymore, and he withdrew from his many successes. This "seesaw" pattern is very common, and Adlerians know how to predict and help this kind of situation because they understand the family dynamics (see also Ferguson, 1958). The point about emotions fitting a purpose was seen clearly with these two boys: whoever was a "winner" and defeated the other was cheerful and pleasant, and whoever was not "superior" was glum and withdrawn. In their deeply competitive strivings for superiority, they believed that only one of them could have a place that was positive and that only one could feel socially useful and belonging. Thus they were both vulnerable. Whoever was "successful" showed one type of emotion and whoever was "defeated" showed the other type of emotion. When success and defeat were reversed, so were the emotions of the two boys. The purpose of the emotions was to move each boy in the direction in which he was oriented. When he moved toward "success" he had socially positive emotions, and when he moved toward "uselessness" he had socially negative emotions, which reflected his belief that "if I can't find recognition by 'success' I'll find my place be being 'terrible' and a failure." Emotions move us toward closeness with others or they help us maintain distance from others. When we seek love and friendship we have different emotions than when we seek power and combat. Because in our society the common belief is that emotions are caused by outside forces, we rarely recognize that emotions are an outgrowth of our own choices and decisions.

A very good illustration of the purposiveness of emotions is provided by "guilt feelings." Such a type of emotion is experienced by many persons and generally involves discomfort and even distress. Although remorse may be felt, a more prominent aspect is the attitude of "what a bad person I am." The outstanding characteristics of "guilt feelings" are that they focus on the past and that they are concerned with the individual's own status. The individual with guilt feelings does not have a problem-solving future orientation that is concerned with "what can I do to improve the situation." Guilt feelings represent a self-oriented emotion which focuses on one's own status as a wrong-doer rather than representing a concern for the welfare of the other person whom one has wronged. In an important paper titled "Guilt feelings as an excuse", Dreikurs (1967) clarified that guilt feelings need to be distinguished from guilt. When experiencing "guilt feelings" the person on the one hand pursues private gains that are counter to Social Interest and on the other hand seeks to demonstrate his or her good intentions. Dreikurs pointed out that although guilt feelings purport to show a high moral sense, they are in fact a substitute for responsible actions. The good intentions are a smoke screen for avoiding doing what the person knows to be responsible behavior. The guilt feelings indicate "a present discouragement seeking proof in the past to justify a feeling of worthlessness or inadequacy" and they focus on "actual or imagined past faulty actions for the purpose of justifying present mistaken attitudes" (Dreikurs, 1967, p.234).

In distinguishing guilt from *guilt feelings,* Dreikurs pointed out that persons who have guilt and realize their mistakes in the past do not necessarily develop guilt feelings, and in fact the individual "who is sincere in his regret does not develop guilt feelings, but tries to correct and amend what he has done" (Dreikurs, 1967, p.234). Moreover, guilt feelings do not assure that the same misbehavior won't occur again. When the person makes sincere efforts to atone or amend, the guilt feelings will disappear. Since the purpose of the guilt feelings is to avoid responsible actions, once action is taken the guilt feelings are no longer necessary. Sometimes a person cannot atone for past misdeeds, since sometimes history cannot be undone. If one feels guilty for events that cannot be rectified, one needs to accept the past realistically. One also needs to accept the fact that one can learn from past mistakes. Of importance for understanding guilt feelings is that the person purposely looks for past misdeeds in order to avoid tasks that he or she is faced with at the present time. The person with guilt feelings "does not feel sorry for what he has done, but rather for what must be endured right now" (Dreikurs, 1967, p.235).

Because guilt feelings give the appearance of a concern with duty and social responsibility, neither other persons nor the individual himself tend to recognize that the purpose of guilt feelings is to evade solving difficulties of the moment. The person does not choose a problem-solving orientation, because he feels inadequate in dealing with present demands. A preoccupation with one's prestige pre-empts meeting the problems of the present time; in looking for past misdeeds the person justifies his failure to meet present problems.

Guilt feelings illustrate how emotions serve a purpose. Moreover, guilt feelings illustrate the way conscience can be manifested. Adlerians share the point of view generally held by laymen and professionals alike, that conscience is the internationalization of rules and ethics learned by the person from his family and culture. Conscience involves both knowledge and acceptance of values and rules regarding human conduct and relationships. At any given moment a person may choose not to follow these internalized beliefs. If the individual accepts these beliefs only in order to fend off punishment from powerful others, then he is likely to behave in line with his conscience only to a limited extent and only according to the given, immediate, circumstances. Such an individual will be more concerned with his or her own prestige than with the welfare of others, and when the person's prestige is threatened, the dictates of conscience are also likely to be discarded. However, if a person chooses not to be openly defiant, by means of guilt feelings he or she can assert "I have a conscience." Many persons, of course, accept the internalized beliefs of conscience as a result of their own world view and their genuine concern for others, and not because they fear punishment or fear reprisal for failure to conform to the commonly accepted rules and values. Such persons are likely to guide their actions according to their conscience. Such persons also are likely to assume full responsibility for their actions and choices, rather than to rely on excuses or to blame factors outside themselves.

Rather than accept the idea that the person himself decides what action to take, many people consider that conscience or emotions *make* us do things. A common statement is "my conscience won't let me do this", or, "my emotions make me do this." In their firm belief that conscience and emotion have a force of their own, many people have difficulty accepting the Adlerian view, that emotion and conscience are used in line with one's purpose. Both emotion and conscience are vital for human actions. But they do not control us. We can learn to dispense with such statements as "my emotions got the best of me" or "the spirit was willing but the flesh was weak" or "forces beyond me control my action." We can learn, instead, to say "I made the decision, I made the choice, and I accept whatever consequences will follow."

CHAPTER 8

NATURAL AND LOGICAL CONSEQUENCES, PSYCHOPATHOLOGY, AND COUNSELING

When children are brought up to learn the natural consequences of their own as well as other people's behavior, this learning has long-term positive effects with far-reaching implications. Effective decision making becomes possible when one knows the consequences of one's actions. Moreover, being able to predict cause-and-effect relationships in human conduct helps a person to have confidence in his judgment and to be willing to take responsibility for his own actions. When children understand the effects of their behavior on others and when they realize what consequences occur from their choices and decisions, they are likely to gain a perspective which permits them to discern order and pattern in human affairs. Such children are not likely to develop a world view in which life is chaos and in which each of us is an innocent victim of circumstances.

The application of Adlerian principles to human relationships emphasizes natural and logical consequences rather than authoritarian control of outcomes. In raising children, parents are encouraged to follow democratic methods that train the child how to participate in decision making. Not only does this give-and-take in the home help the child to realize his own value as a contributing member, but the child learns to predict outcomes, to recognize his own plans and decisions, and to find effective ways for modifying his behavior. The more the child experiences order rather than caprice, the more likely he is to interpret events around him in a realistic fashion and to trust his own decision making. What is true about raising children is also valid for other types of human relationships. In marriage, the more the partners share in decisions and experience the natural outcomes of their actions, the better will they learn to anticipate difficulties, and the less likely will they be to misinterpret each other or to feel victimized by the partner. Likewise in the work place, the more the boss permits participation in decision making and lets natural consequences rather than arbitrary authority determine outcomes of actions, the more likely will be the spirit of cooperation and trust among employees.

Rewards and punishments that come from external sources in an arbitrary fashion do not teach a person to rely on his or her own judgment and resources. Externally administered rewards and punishments may temporarily alter specific behaviors but they do not teach self-confidence, self-reliance, or courage to be creative and to contribute. Adlerians stress encouragement instead of reward, since effective learning requires the individual to recognize and utilize his own strength. Encouragement helps to increase someone's courage; reward alters specific behavior for a given moment. Courage brings self-reliance even in the face of limited external environmental support, while rewarding individuals for good behavior teaches the person to rely on the external environment rather than to trust his own judgment and strength. Adlerian methods of training, counseling, and guidance emphasize the use of encouragement rather than rewards, and logical and natural consequences* rather than punishment. These methods apply equally in the home, the school, and the workplace. They are part of a democratic process of interacting with others and they show respect for the individual. Neither autocratic methods nor laissez faire methods help the individual function with confidence, since the autocratic methods show no respect for the individual and the laissez faire methods fail to provide the sense of order that is needed for self-confidence and effective decision making.

Individuals who were raised with either laissez faire or autocratic methods are likely to exaggerate their own weaknesses and are likely to magnify either the unhelpfulness or the powerfulness of others. Such individuals grow up not trusting themselves nor trusting others. When persons doubt their own strength and apperceive life as uncaring or unfair, they will tend to find a myriad of excuses for not meeting life demands. A negative bias based on distorted assessment of actual life circumstances blocks the individual from finding solutions to problems and predisposes the person to withdraw and give up rather than to seek ways of improving his situation.

Failure to participate fully in the give-and-take of social living is what Adler described as characteristic of psychopathology. From an Adlerian perspective, psychopathology is fundamentally a disturbance in attitude, a false belief regarding one's own limitations and a mistaken set of ideas about life. These mistaken beliefs prevent the neurotic, psychotic, and criminal from full participation and contribution. Psychopathology manifests itself in the way the person deals with work, marriage, and friendship (what Adler called "the three tasks of life"**). Feeling inadequate, and perceiving the world as unjust, unpredictable, or outright malevolent, the individual neurotic, psychotic, or criminal shuns cooperation and avoids solving real-life problems. The psychopathological process need not result in a fully-developed illness or criminality, for Adler recognized a continuity between optimum positive attitudes and extreme discouragement and disillusionment. Psychopathology and "healthy functioning" are not either-or, all-or-none, dichotomies, but instead form a continuum.

The diminished functioning in psychopathology does not come from genuine ineptness or lack of knowledge so much as from an attitude of "I won't play ball, or if I do, I'll play only by *my* rules." The diminished functioning represents not merely a failure to cooperate and to contribute, but comes from a *refusal* to cooperate and to contribute. In believing that full participation is not possible, that life is futile and that his efforts will bring no improvements, the individual in his discouragement refuses to meet life demands and refuses to find ways of contributing.***

Through encouragement and re-education, Adlerians have helped individuals to reduce or eliminate their psychopathological beliefs and modes of living. Because Adler viewed psychopathology in terms of mistaken attitudes and beliefs, he considered therapy and counseling to be a form of education, one that helps the person learn new attitudes and beliefs. Adlerian principles therefore

---

* Dreikurs (Dreikurs, Grunwald, & Pepper, 1971/1982; Dreikurs & Cassel, 1972) distinguished between natural and logical consequences and between courage and bravado. The interested reader may wish to read the way Dreikurs draws these distinctions.

** Mosak and Dreikurs described these three "tasks" and added a fourth and fifth life task (Dreikurs & Mosak, 1966; 1967; Mosak & Dreikurs, 1967).

*** Further reading is recommended, such as the papers by K.A. Adler (1961) on depression, by Shulman and Mosak 1967) on the purpose of symptoms, and the book by Shulman (1968) on schizophrenia.

apply equally in raising children, teaching pupils in school, and providing counseling and psychotherapy to persons who seek help in an office or who are in hospitals or prisons. Through re-education, the individual in psychotherapy and counseling learns to have new concepts about himself and other persons. Instead of finding excuses or blaming outside factors, the individual learns to take note of how his actions bring about specific consequences. By recognizing what effect the person has on others and on tasks at hand, the person comes to realize that he is not as helpless or as weak as he formerly believed. With psychotherapy and counseling the person comes to the realization that as he changes his behavior, the external world becomes more supportive and less malevolent. By learning to recognize the consequences of his own actions and decisions, the person comes to believe that he has choices and alternatives. As a result of encouragement, he learns to believe that by means of his own strength and creativeness he can participate and contribute, and that he can live a more satisfying and full life.

REFERENCES

Adler, A. **What life should mean to you.** New York: Putnam Capricorn Books, 1958. (Originally published in 1931).

Adler, K.A. Depression in the light of Individual Psychology. **Journal of Individual Psychology,** 1961, **17,** 56-67.

Bottome, P. **Alfred Adler: A portrait from life.** New York: Vanguard Press, 1957. (Originally published in 1939).

Dreikurs, R. The four goals of the maladjusted child. **Nervous Child,** 1947, **6,** 321-328.

Dreikurs, R. **The challenge of parenthood.** New York: Hawthorn, 1948.

Dreikurs, R. **Fundamentals of Adlerian psychology.** Chicago: Alfred Adler Institute, 1953. (Originally published in English in 1950.)

Dreikurs, R. **Psychology in the classroom.** New York: Harper, 1957.

Dreikurs, R. The psychological uncertainty principle. **Topical Problems in Psychotherapy,** 1963, **4,** 23-31.

Dreikurs, R. Guilt feelings as an excuse. In R. Dreikurs (Ed.), **Psychodynamics, psychotherapy, and counseling.** Chicago: Alfred Adler Institute, 1967.

Dreikurs, R. **Grundbegriffe der Individualpsychologie.** (Revised edition of Fundamentals of Individual Psychology). Stuttgart: Ernst Klett, 1969.

Dreikurs, R. **Social equality: The challenge of today.** Chicago: Alfred Adler Institute, 1983. (Originally published in 1971.)

Dreikurs, R., & Cassel, P. **Discipline without tears.** New York: Hawthorn, 1972.

Dreikurs, R., Grunwald, B.B., & Pepper, F.C. **Maintaining sanity in the classroom: Illustrated teaching techniques.** Second Edition. New York: Harper & Row, 1982. (Originally published in 1971).

Dreikurs, R., & Mosak, H.H. The life tasks I. Adler's three tasks. **Individual Psychologist,** 1966, **4,** 18-22.

Dreikurs, R., & Mosak, H.H. The life tasks II. The fourth life task. **Individual Psychologist,** 1967, **4,** 51-56.

Dreikurs, R., & Soltz, V. **Children: The challenge.** New York: Hawthorn, 1964.

Ferguson, E.D. The effect of sibling competition and alliance on level of aspiration, expectation, and performance. **Journal of Abnormal and Social Psychology,** 1958, **56,** 213-222.

Ferguson, E.D. The use of early recollections in assessing life style and diagnosing psychopathology. **Journal of Projective Techniques and Personality Assessment,** 1964, **28,** 403-412.

Ferguson, E.D. Adlerian psychology, Social Interest, and motivation theory. In T. Reinelt, Z. Otálora, & H. Kappus (Eds.), **Die Begegnung der Individualpsychologie mit anderen Therapieformen.** (The encounter of Individual Psychology with other forms of therapy). Munich: Reinhardt, 1984.

McClelland, D.C. Risk taking in children with high and low need for achievement. In J.W. Atkinson (Ed.), **Motives in fantasy, action, and society.** New York: Van Nostrand, 1958.

McClelland, D.C. **The achieving society.** New York: Van Nostrand, 1961.

McClelland, D.C. What is the effect of achievement motivation training in the schools? In D.C. McClelland & R.S. Steele (Eds.), **Human motivation: A book of readings.** Morristown, NJ: General Learning Press, 1973.

Mosak, H.H. Early recollections as a projective technique. **Journal of Projective Techniques,** 1958, **22,** 302-311.

Mosak, H.H., & Dreikurs, R. The life tasks III. The fifth life task. **Individual Psychologist,** 1967, **5,** 16-22.

Murray, H. **Explorations in personality.** New York: Oxford University Press, 1938.

Orgler, H. **Alfred Adler: The man and his work, triumph over the inferiority complex.** (4th ed.). London: Sidgwick and Jackson, 1973. (Originally published in 1939.)

Piaget, J. **The origin of intelligence in the child.** London: Routledge, 1953.

Piaget, J. **The child's construction of intelligence.** London: Routledge, 1955.

Shulman, B. **Essays in schizophrenia.** Baltimore, MD: Williams & Wilkins, 1968.

Shulman, B. & Mosak, H. Various purposes of symptoms. **Journal of Individual Psychology,** 1967, **23,** 79-87.

Sicher, L. Education for freedom. **American Journal of Individual Psychology,** 1955, **11,** 97-103.

Way, L. **Adler's place in psychology: An exposition of Individual Psychology.** New York: Collier, 1962. (Originally published in 1949).

Wiener, N. Time, communication, and the nervous system. In L.K. Frank (Ed.), Teleological mechanisms. **Annals of the New York Academy of Sciences,** 1948, **50,** 187-278.

BOOKS AND PAPERS SUGGESTED FOR READING

Adler, A. **The education of children.** London: Allen & Unwin, 1957.

Adler, A. Feeling and emotions from the standpoint of Individual Psychology. In M. Reymert (Ed.), **The Wittenberg Symposium.** Worcester, Mass: Clark University Press, 1928.

Adler, A. **Practice and theory of Individual Psychology.** New York: Humanitas Press, 1927/1971.

Adler, A. **Problems of neurosis.** New York: Harper & Row, 1964.

Adler, A. **The science of living.** New York: Anchor Books, 1929/1969.

Adler, A. **Social Interest: A challenge to mankind.** New York: Putnam, 1939.

Adler, K.A. Depression in the light of Individual Psychology. **Journal of Individual Psychology,** 1961, **17,** 56-67.

Dreikurs, R., & Soltz, V. **Children: The challenge.** New York: Hawthorn, 1964/1967.

Dreikurs, R. **The challenge of child training: A parent's guide.** New York: Hawthorn, 1972.

Dreikurs, R. **The challenge of marriage.** New York: Hawthorn, 1946.

Dreikurs, R. **The challenge of parenthood.** New York: Hawthorn, 1948/1958.

Dreikurs, R. Family counseling: A demonstration. **Journal of Individual Psychology,** 1972, **28,** 202-222.

Dreikurs, R. The four goals of children's misbehavior. **Nervous Child,** 1947, **6,** 3-11.

Dreikurs, R. The function of emotions. In R. Dreikurs (Ed.), **Psychodynamics, psychotherapy, and counseling.** Chicago: Alfred Adler Institute, 1967.

Dreikurs, R. **Fundamentals of Adlerian Psychology.** Chicago: Alfred Adler Institute, 1950/1953.

Dreikurs, R. **Group psychotherapy and group approaches: Collected papers.** Chicago: Alfred Adler Institute, 1960.

Dreikurs, R. Group psychotherapy from the point of view of Adlerian psychology. **International Journal of Group Psychotherapy,** 1957, **7,** 363-375.

Dreikurs, R. **Prevention and correction of juvenile delinquency.** Chicago: Alfred Adler Institute, 1962.

Dreikurs, R. **Psychodynamics, psychotherapy, and counseling: Collected papers.** Chicago: Alfred Adler Institute, 1967.

Dreikurs, R. The psychological interview in medicine. **American Journal of Individual Psychology,** 1954, **10,** 99-122.

Dreikurs, R. **Psychology in the classroom.** New York: Harper & Row, 1957/1968.

Dreikurs, R. **Social equality: The challenge of today.** Chicago: Alfred Adler Institute, 1971/1983.

Dreikurs, R., Rudolf Dreikurs Bibliography: 1925-1967. **Journal of Individual Psychology,** 1967, **23,** 158-166.

Dreikurs, R., Corsini, R.J., Lowe, R., & Sonstegard, M. **Adlerian family counseling.** Eugene, Oreg: University of Oregon Press, 1959.

Dreikurs, R., & Dinkmeyer, D. **Encouraging children to learn: The encouragement process.** Englewood Cliffs, N.J.: Prentice-Hall, 1963.

Dreikurs, R., Gould, S., & Corsini, R.J., **Family council: The Dreikurs technique for putting an end to the war between parents and children.** Chicago: Regnery, 1974.

Dreikurs, R., & Grey, L. **Logical consequences: A new approach to discipline.** New York: Meredith, 1968.

Dreikurs, R., Grunwald, B.B., & Pepper, F.C. **Maintaining sanity in the classroom: Illustrated teaching techniques.** New York: Harper & Row, 1971/1982.

Dreikurs, R., & Mosak, H.H. The life tasks II. The fourth life task. **Individual Psychologist,** 1967, **4,** 51-56.

Ferguson, E.D. The use of early recollections for assessing life style and diagnosing psychopathology. **Journal of Projective Techniques and Personality Assessment,** 1964, **28,** 403-412.

Ferguson, E.D. The effect of sibling competition and alliance on level of aspiration, expectation, and performance. **Journal of Abnormal and Social Psychology,** 1958, **56,** 213 222.

Feguson, E.D. Rudolf Dreikurs Bibliography: 1967-1972. **Journal of Individual Psychology,** 1973, **29,** 19-23.

Fiedler, F.E. A comparison of therapeutic relationships in psychoanalytic, nondirective and Adlerian therapies. **Journal of Consulting Psychology,** 1950, **14,** 436-445.

Mosak, H.H. **Alfred Adler: His influence on psychology today.** Park Ridge, IL: Noyes Press, 1973.

Mosak, H.H., & Dreikurs, R. Adlerian psychotherapy. In R.J. Corsini (Ed.), **Current Psychotherapies.** Itasca, IL: Peacock, 1973.

Mosak, H.H. Early recollections as a projective technique. **Journal of Projective Techniques,** 1958, **22,** 302-311.

Mosak, H.H. **On purpose: Collected papers.** Chicago: Alfred Adler Institute, 1977.

Shulman, B. & Mosak, H. Various purposes of symptoms. **Journal of Individual Psychology,** 1967, **23,** 79-87.

Shulman, B. **Essays in schizophrenia.** Baltimore, MD: Williams & Wilkins, 1968.

Shulman, B. The family constellation in personality diagnosis. **Journal of Individual Psychology,** 1962, **18,** 35-47.

NOTES

22059818R00026